Magnetism

by Grace Hansen

Abdo Kids Jumbo is an Imprint of Abdo Kids
abdopublishing.com

abdopublishing.com

Published by Abdo Kids, a division of ABDO, P.O. Box 398166, Minneapolis, Minnesota 55439.
Copyright © 2019 by Abdo Consulting Group, Inc. International copyrights reserved in all countries.
No part of this book may be reproduced in any form without written permission from the publisher.
Abdo Kids Jumbo™ is a trademark and logo of Abdo Kids.

052018

092018

 THIS BOOK CONTAINS
RECYCLED MATERIALS

Photo Credits: iStock, Shutterstock

Production Contributors: Teddy Borth, Jennie Forsberg, Grace Hansen

Design Contributors: Dorothy Toth, Laura Mitchell

Library of Congress Control Number: 2017960572

Publisher's Cataloging-in-Publication Data

Names: Hansen, Grace, author.

Title: Magnetism / by Grace Hansen.

Description: Minneapolis, Minnesota : Abdo Kids, 2019. | Series: Beginning science |
    Includes glossary, index and online resources (page 24).

Identifiers: ISBN 9781532108105 (lib.bdg.) | ISBN 9781532109089 (ebook) |
    ISBN 9781532109577 (Read-to-me ebook)

Subjects: LCSH: Magnetism--Juvenile literature. | Physics--Juvenile literature. |
    Magnets--Juvenile literature.

Classification: DDC 538--dc23

Table of Contents

What Is a Magnet?. 4

North & South Poles 14

A Giant Magnet 18

Let's Review! 22

Glossary 23

Index 24

Abdo Kids Code. 24

What Is a Magnet?

A magnet is a material or object that has a force. This force attracts certain materials, like iron.

4

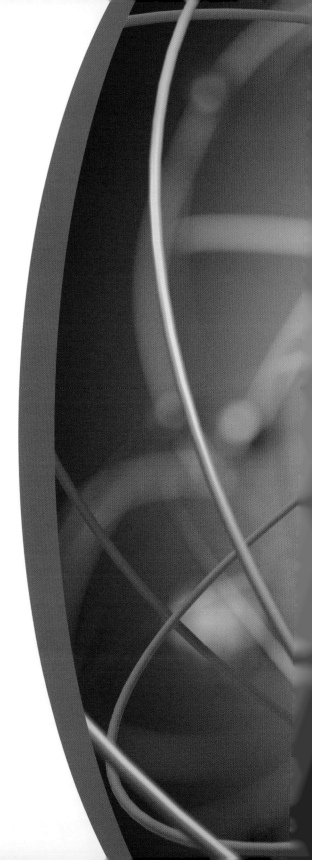

Most non-magnetic materials have atoms with paired **electrons**. The electrons move in opposite directions.

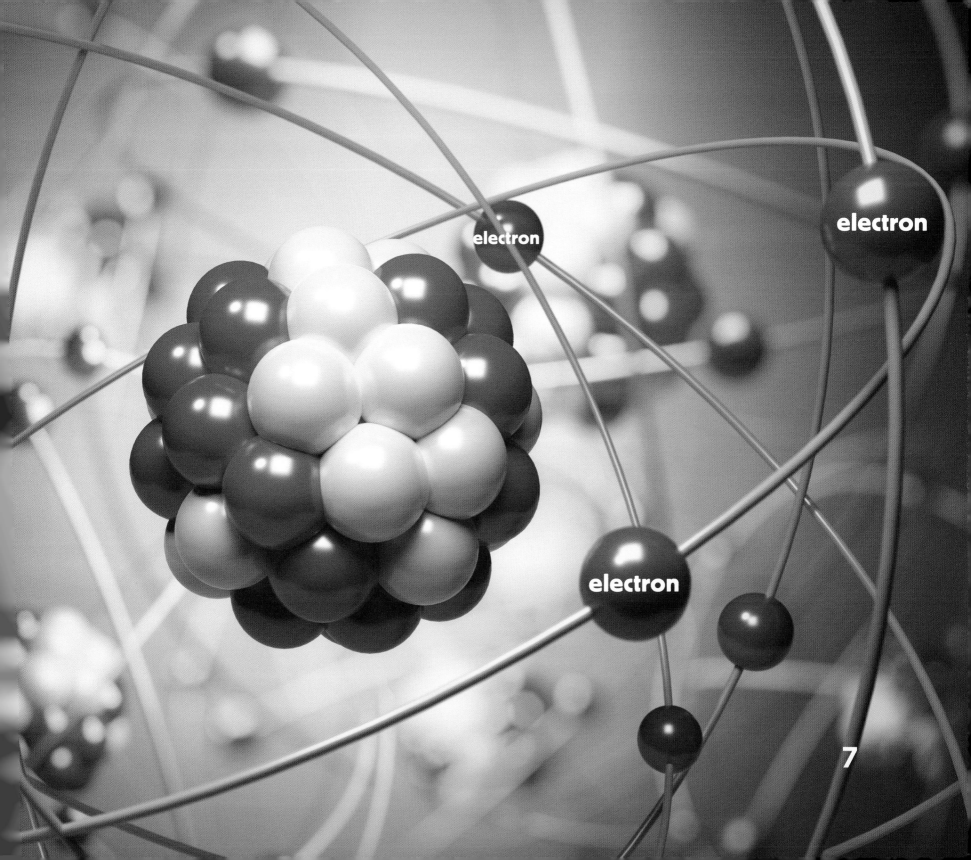

electron

electron

electron

7

Iron is often magnetic. An iron atom has four unpaired **electrons**. These electrons spin **parallel** to one another.

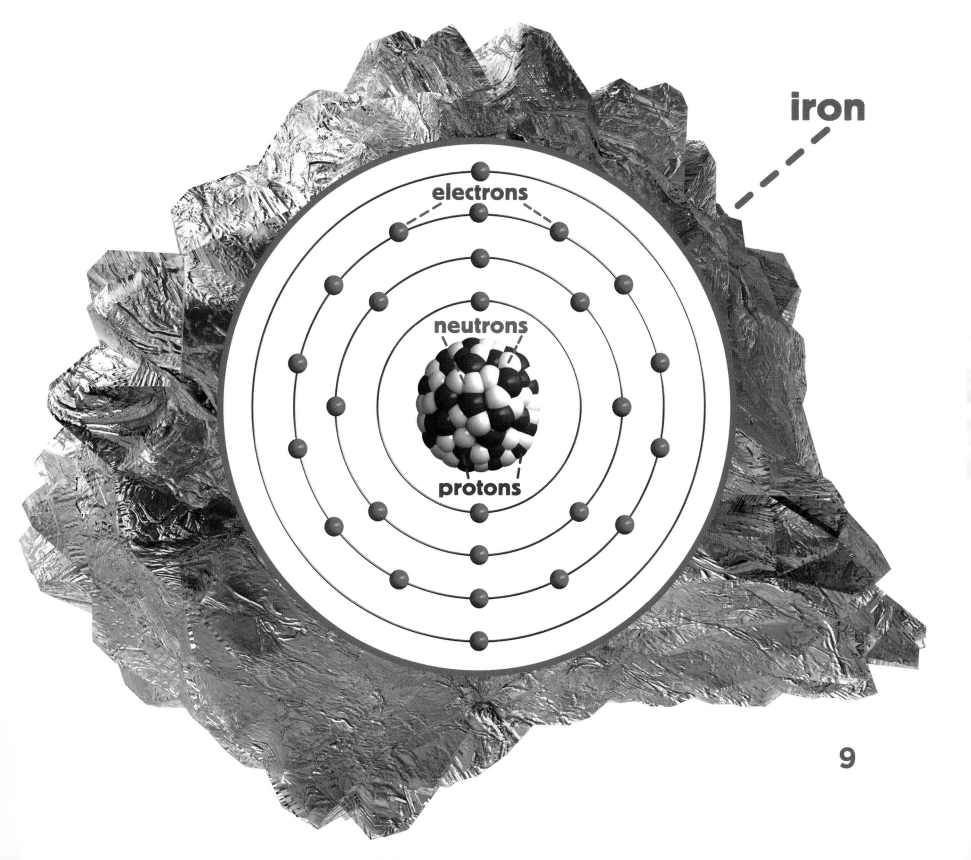

iron

electrons

neutrons

protons

9

Electrons are like tiny particles of electricity. Magnetism is made by flowing electricity. When electrons flow inside an atom it creates a magnetic field.

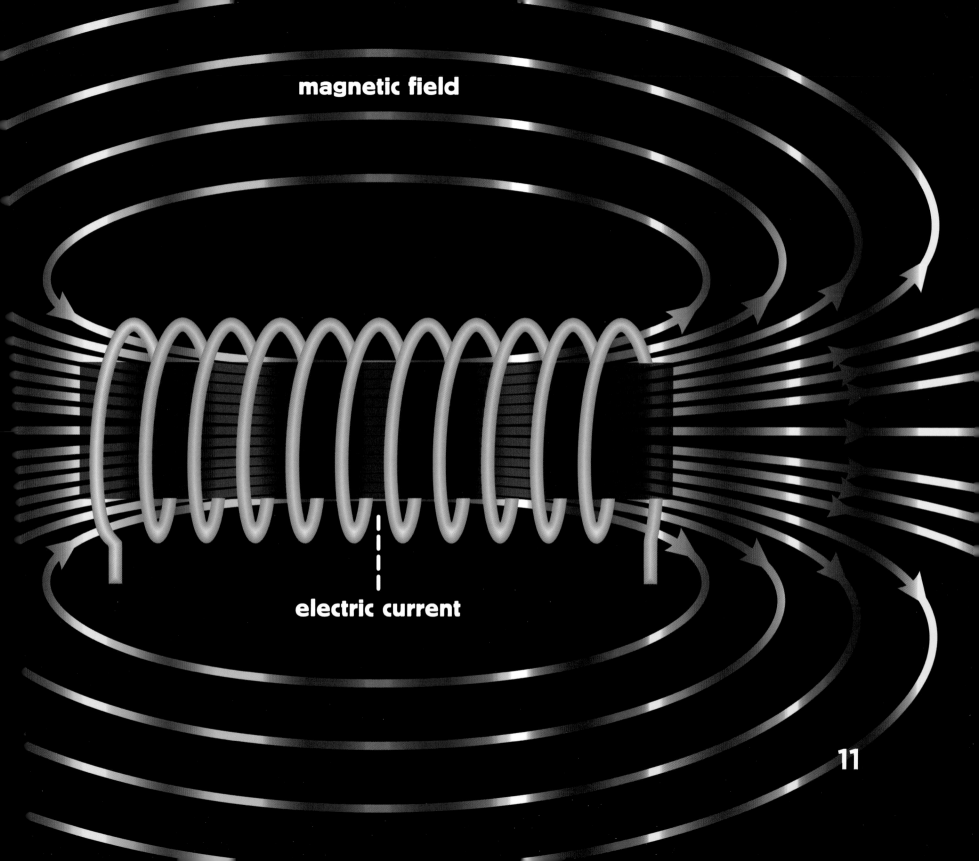

A magnet has a magnetic field. We cannot see it. But we can see it working.

North & South Poles

A magnet has a north and a south pole. The magnet is strongest at these poles.

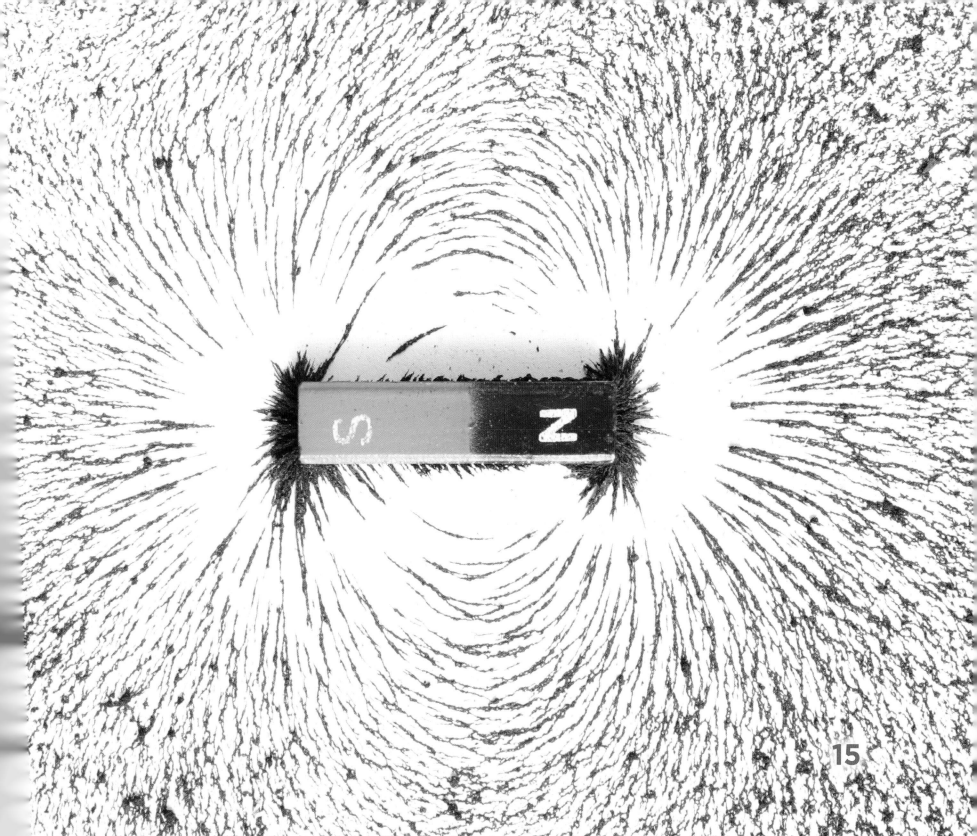

15

If two magnets are put near each other, they interact. The north and south poles attract. Like poles repel each other.

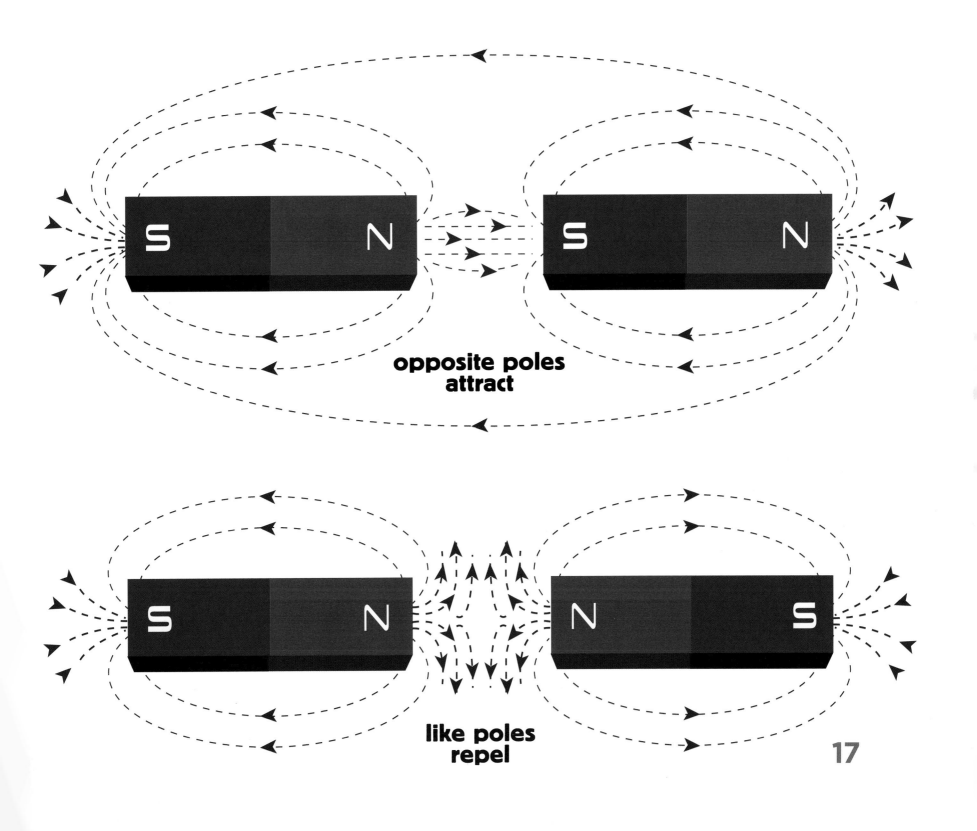

opposite poles
attract

like poles
repel

17

A Giant Magnet

The Earth is a giant magnet.

Inside Earth is **molten rock**

rich in magnetic materials.

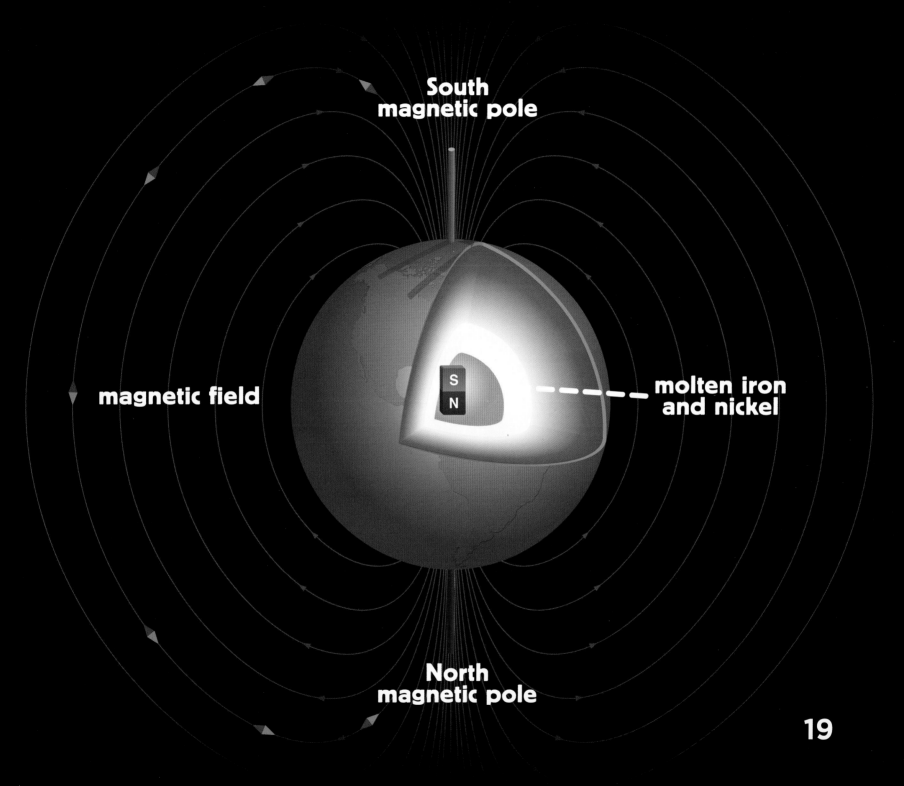

South
magnetic pole

magnetic field

S
N

molten iron
and nickel

North
magnetic pole

19

This means that Earth has a magnetic field! It stretches out into space. It protects us from most of the charged particles the sun fires off!

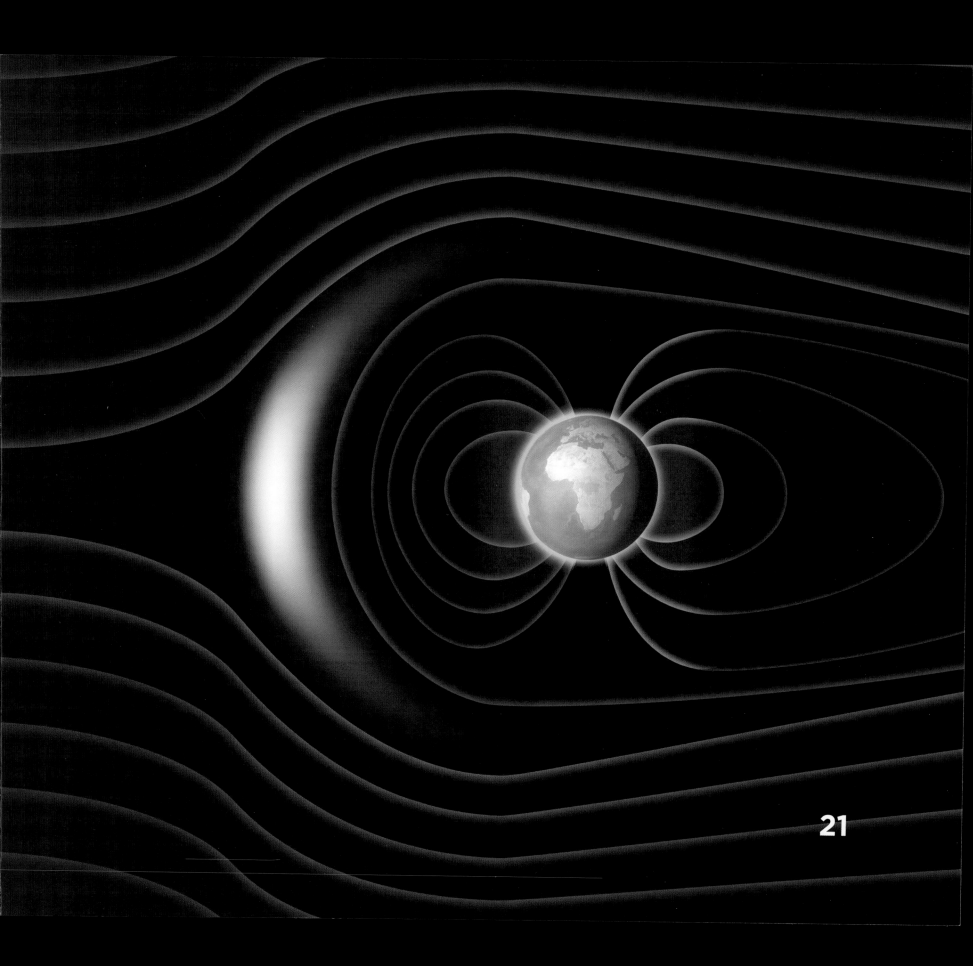

Let's Review!

- Magnetism is an invisible **force**.

- A magnet has a magnetic field that flows from its north and south poles.

- Most objects have **electrons** that spin in opposite directions. Magnets have electrons that spin in the same direction.

- Earth is a giant magnet. It has a north and south pole. There is magnetic material in its core.

Glossary

charged particle – a particle with an electric charge.

electron – a very small particle that moves outside the nucleus of an atom. Electrons have a negative charge.

force – a push or pull upon an object that happens when another object acts on it.

molten rock – rock that has been melted.

parallel – moving in the same direction, being the same distance apart at every point, and never crossing each other.

repel – to force back.

23

Index

atom 6, 8

Earth 18, 20

electricity 10

electron 6, 8, 10

iron 4, 8

magnetic field 10, 12, 20

poles 14, 16

sun 20

Abdo Kids
ONLINE
FREE! ONLINE MULTIMEDIA RESOURCES

Visit **abdokids.com** and use this code to access crafts, games, videos, and more!

Abdo Kids Code:
BMK8105